THE ANIMALS OF ASIA

CAMELS

WILLOW CLARK

PowerKiDS
press™

New York

Published in 2013 by The Rosen Publishing Group, Inc.
29 East 21st Street, New York, NY 10010

First Edition

Editor: Joanne Randolph
Book Design: Ashley Drago
Layout Design: Julio Gil

Library of Congress Cataloging-in-Publication Data

Clark, Willow.
 Camels / by Willow Clark. — 1st ed.
    p. cm. — (The animals of asia)
 Includes index.
 ISBN 978-1-4488-7416-3 (library binding) — ISBN 978-1-4488-7489-7 (pbk.) —
ISBN 978-1-4488-7563-4 (6-pack)
 1. Camels—Juvenile literature. I. Title.
 QL737.U54C53 2013
 599.63'62—dc23

                                        2011051477

Manufactured in China

CPSIA Compliance Information: Batch #WKTS12PK: For Further Information contact Rosen Publishing, New York, New York at 1-800-237-9932

CONTENTS

HELLO, CAMEL!

Camels are large **mammals** that are native to the deserts of North Africa, the Middle East, and Asia. There are two **species**, or types, of camels. The dromedary camel lives in North Africa and the Middle East. The Bactrian camel lives in central Asia.

◀ Many people think camels live only in hot, dry deserts. This wild camel lives in the Gobi, a desert in Mongolia, where temperatures can fall as low as -40° F (-40° C) in the winter.

Most of the camels living today are **domesticated**. That means that they have been raised to live among people and to do work for them. Camels have been so important to desert transportation that they are sometimes called the ships of the desert. This book will introduce you to these important Asian animals.

Bactrian camels like these are the only wild camels left. However, most Bactrians are domesticated, just as dromedaries are.

WHERE IN THE WORLD?

Dromedary camels live in the deserts of North Africa, parts of India, and the western part of Asia called the Middle East. The climate throughout their range is hot year-round and very dry outside of a short rainy season. There are also **feral** dromedaries that live in Australia's desert. Feral animals are

Camels are well suited to life in dry, hot places. Their feet are wide to help them walk in sand. They can also go a long time without food or water. ▼

These camels live in Mongolia. Bactrian camels grow thick fur in the winter to keep warm. They then shed this fur once the weather gets warmer. ▼

domesticated animals that have returned to the wild. These feral dromedaries came from the camels that were brought to Australia to work in the nineteenth century!

Bactrian camels have a much smaller range than dromedary camels. They live in the deserts in northwestern China and southern Mongolia. The climate there is also dry. The temperature can be very cold or very hot, depending on the time of year.

AT HOME IN THE DESERT

Camels have been domesticated for over 3,000 years. There are people living in desert habitats who use camels to do jobs similar to those that horses do. Camels' bodies can deal with harsher climates than horses', though. The deserts where camels live can be more than 120° F (49° C) in the summer!

Camels can live even after losing 30 percent of their bodies' water. Other animals would die after losing just 15 percent.

Here a dromedary camel pulls a cart in India. Camels have been domesticated animals for thousands of years.

Both dromedary and Bactrian camels have been domesticated. About 90 percent of domestic camels are dromedaries, though. The only truly wild camels left in the world are wild Bactrian camels. Wild Bactrian camels are very rare. It is thought that there are fewer than 1,000 left, which makes them a critically **endangered** species. This means that they could soon die out completely.

ONE HUMP OR TWO?

The easiest way to tell the two camel species apart is to look at their humps. Dromedary camels have one hump, while Bactrian camels have two.

◀ A Bactrian camel can go a week or longer without water. When water becomes available, it can drink 30 gallons (114 l) in just a few minutes!

You might think that a camel's humps store water. This is not true, though. Camels' humps are fat stores. A hump can store up to 80 pounds (36 kg) of fat, which the animal can break down and use for energy when food is scarce. This means camels do not have to eat or drink every day.

11

AMAZING ADAPTATIONS

Camels have many other **adaptations** to desert life besides their humps. Their nostrils trap most of the water in their breath as they breathe out. This water is put back into their bodies, so very little water is lost to the air when they breathe.

Bactrian camels have adaptations to their fur to protect them from the cold winters in central

Camels have two rows of extra long eyelashes to keep desert sands out of their eyes. These long eyelashes also help keep their eyes safe from bright sunlight.

Asia's deserts. Temperatures there can drop to -20° F (-29° C). They grow thicker, shaggier coats for the winter. They shed these coats as the temperature starts to rise. Even camels in hot deserts are helped by their fur. This fur helps keep the Sun's heat away from their bodies.

Heat and blowing sand are part of daily life in the desert. Camels can seal their nostrils shut to keep sand out. ▼

▼ Wide feet with thick footpads help camels keep their footing. They also move both legs on each side of their bodies at the same time. This also helps them walk on sand and rocky land.

13

TIME TO EAT

Camels are **herbivores**. This means that they are plant eaters. Their large, tough lips are split in the middle. This makes it easier for them to eat dry, tough, bitter, or thorny desert plants. Domestic camels eat foods like grasses, grains, and dates.

▼ When camels do drink, they can drink a lot at one time. This is helpful since they live in places where water can be hard to come by!

Camels **digest**, or break down, food similarly to the way that cows do. First they partly chew and swallow their food. This food later comes back up from the stomach. The camel then chews and swallows it one last time. This is called chewing the cud. This kind of digestion helps camels get the most **nutrients** possible out of their food.

DEFENSES AND COMMUNICATION

Did you know that camels sometimes spit? When a camel feels threatened, it will spit a mixture of stomach contents and saliva. This **defense** is meant to surprise the threatening animal and make it go away. Camels may also spit if they get very

▼ The lead male camel leads the caravan from the rear. The females take turns at the front of the caravan.

▲ *Camels communicate with each other by making different sounds, such as groans, bleats, and growls.*

excited. They are generally not aggressive. The closest they get to fighting is pushing or nipping at each other.

Both domestic and wild camels travel together in groups, called caravans. A caravan is made up of a male leader, a few females, and their young.

BABY CAMELS

The camel's **mating** season happens in the fall and winter. During mating season, male camels may fight with each other over females. Males may spit at, bite, or even try to sit on their rivals!

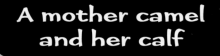

A mother camel and her calf

Camels generally give birth to just one baby at a time. ▶

Baby camels, or calves, are usually born in the spring, about 12 to 14 months after mating. The calf can stand and walk a few hours after birth. The mother **nurses** her calf for about 18 months. The calf reaches adulthood at between three and five years of age. The camel's life span ranges from about 35 to 50 years.

Domesticated baby camels are taught to wear bridles and carry packs at a young age. This way they are ready to work once they are big enough. ▶

19

CAMELS AND PEOPLE

Domesticated camels have long been valued as pack animals. They carry people and loads over long distances in harsh conditions. They can carry a 200-pound (90 kg) pack for up to 25 miles (40 km) each day. People also value camels for their milk, wool, leather, and meat. Their dung is even used for fuel!

Here two men ride camels through the desert near Jaiselmer, India. This Indian city is home to many camel herders. ▼

Although their camels are domesticated, most camel herders allow their animals freedom to roam. This allows the camels to spread out and graze on a wider area of the desert's plant life. Domestic camels depend on herders for their water, so this need draws them back home!

21

BACTRIAN CAMELS IN DANGER

Wild bactrian camels are critically endangered. This means that their numbers have dropped quickly and are expected to drop by 80 percent within the next few generations. Because there are fewer than 1,000 wild Bactrian camels left, they could even become **extinct**, or die out.

Wild Bactrian camels face several threats. They have lost part of their habitat to mining. They also are hunted, both for sport and because in some places they compete with domestic camels for food and water. There are groups working to protect the wild Bactrian camel so that it can continue to exist.

▲ This Bactrian camel lives in Gobi National Park, which is a protected part of the Gobi.

GLOSSARY

ADAPTATIONS (a-dap-TAY-shunz) Changes in animals that help them stay alive.

DEFENSE (dih-FENTS) Something a living thing does that helps keep it safe.

DIGEST (dy-JEST) To break down food so that the body can use it.

DOMESTICATED (duh-MES-tih-kayt-ed) Raised to live with people.

ENDANGERED (in-DAYN-jerd) In danger of no longer living.

EXTINCT (ik-STINGKT) No longer existing.

FERAL (FER-al) An animal that used to live with humans, which has gone back to the wild.

HERBIVORES (ER-buh-vorz) Animals that eat only plants.

MAMMALS (MA-mulz) Warm-blooded animals that have backbones and hair, breathe air, and feed milk to their young.

MATING (MAYT-ing) Coming together to make babies.

NURSES (NURS-ez) When a female feeds her baby milk from her body.

NUTRIENTS (NOO-tree-ents) Food that a living thing needs to live and grow.

SPECIES (SPEE-sheez) One kind of living thing. All people are one species.

INDEX

B
bodies, 8, 12–13

C
climate(s), 6–8

D
desert(s), 4–8, 13

H
habitat(s), 8, 22

J
jobs, 8

M
mammals, 4
Middle East, 4, 6
Mongolia, 7
mother, 19

N
North Africa, 4, 6

P
people, 5, 8, 20

R
range, 6–7

S
season, 6, 18
ships, 5
species, 4, 9–10
summer, 8

T
temperature, 7, 13
transportation, 5
types, 4

W
wild, 7
work, 5

WEBSITES

Due to the changing nature of Internet links, PowerKids Press has developed an online list of websites related to the subject of this book. This site is updated regularly. Please use this link to access the list:
www.powerkidslinks.com/aoa/camel/